Seasons

SUMMER

Belitha Press

Anna Claybourne • Pictures by Stephen Lewis

Belitha Press

First published in the UK in 2001 by
Belitha Press Limited, London House,
Great Eastern Wharf, Parkgate Road,
London SW11 4NQ

Copyright © Belitha Press Limited 2001
Text by Anna Claybourne

ISBN 1 84138 321 X

British Library Cataloguing in Publication Data for this book is available from the British Library.

Printed in Hong Kong

10 9 8 7 6 5 4 3 2 1

Editor: Veronica Ross
Designer: Kathryn Caulfield
Illustrator: Stephen Lewis
Picture researcher: Juliet Duff
Consultant: Elizabeth Atkinson

Photo credits
Collections: front cover & 4 Sandra Lousada; 7 bottom Anthea Sieveking; 22 bottom Richard Davis; 27 top Fiona Pragoff.
FLPA: 11 top R. Thompson; 12 centre Roger Hosking; 13 Roger Wilmshurst; 15 centre E.T. Scott; 15 bottom F. Merlet; 16 top B. Borrell Casals; 18 top David T Grewcock.
Getty One Stone: 12 top Ron Boardman; 15 centre Ben Osborne; 16 centre Bruce Hands; 16 bottom Bruce Foster; 21 bottom Stuart Westmorland; 25 top Greg Probst; 26 bottom Lori Adamski Peek.
Robert Harding Picture Library: 18 bottom.
Mountain Camera: 9 bottom Colin Monteath.
Powerstock/Zefa: 11 bottom; 23. top Hoa-Qui.
Rex Features: 20 Riku Isohella.
Science Photo Library: 5 top David Parker.
Still Pictures: 9 top mark Edwards; 25 bottom Gil Moti.

Every attempt has been made to clear copyrights but should there be inadvertent omissions please apply to the publisher for rectification.

Contents

Words in **bold** are explained
on pages 30 and 31.

What is summer?

Summer is the hottest time of the year. It's sunny and warm, and the air is full of buzzing insects and the smell of flowers.

Spring

In summer, schools close for the long summer holidays. It's time to play! People go on holiday to the seaside. Roads, railways and airports are very busy.

Summer is a time for going outdoors. You can go for a walk, play games or paddle at the seaside.

summer fact

You should never look directly at the Sun. It could damage your eyes or even blind you.

4

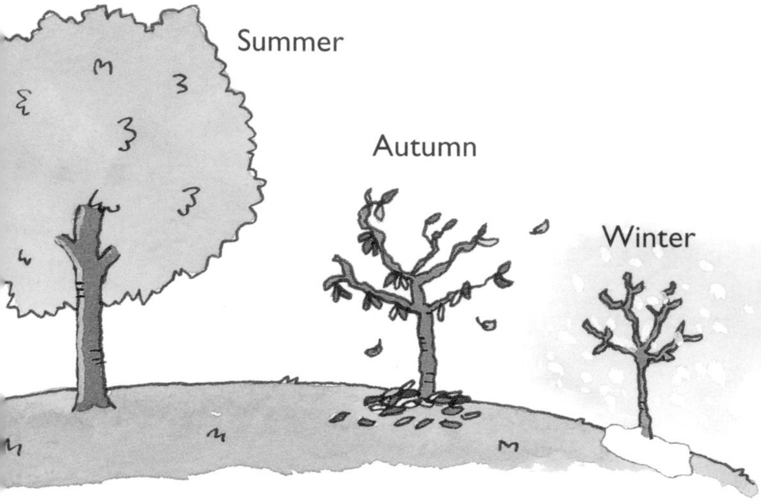

Summer

Autumn

Winter

Red poppies **bloom** in summer. Sometimes there are so many of them, they look like a red carpet.

Summer is one of the four seasons: spring, summer, autumn and winter. Together the four seasons make up the whole year.

Flowers bloom and bees buzz around them, collecting **nectar** and **pollen**. The trees are covered with lush, green leaves. They give shade from the hot Sun.

5

How summer happens

Wherever you live, summer is warmer than any other season. But do you know why?

The Earth is always moving around the Sun in a big circle. It takes a whole year to travel all the way around.

The Earth is tilted to one side. As it moves round the Sun, the tilt makes different parts of the Earth face the Sun at different times. This is why we have seasons.

This picture shows the seasons in the **northern hemisphere**.

Summer happens when the part of the Earth you live in leans towards the Sun.

Winter happens when your part of the Earth is leaning away from the Sun.

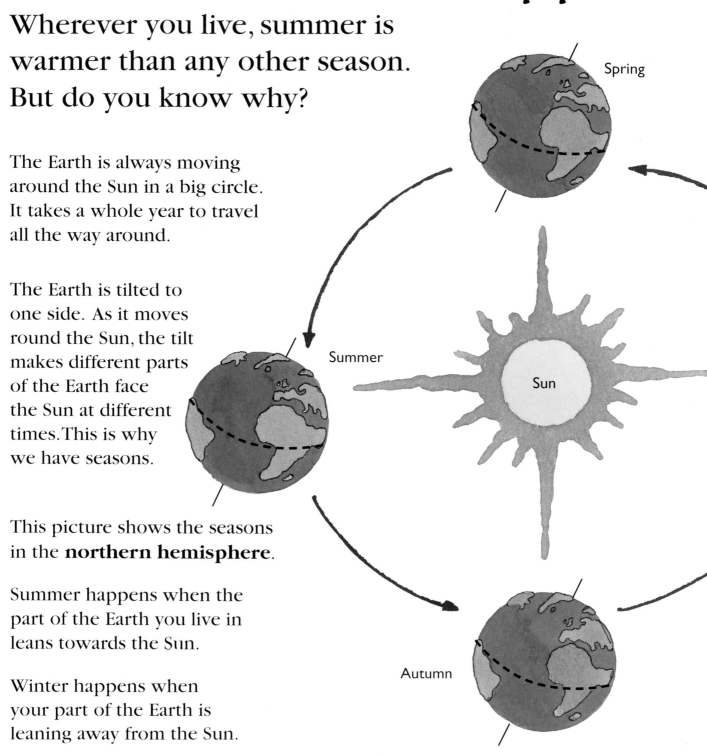

Spring

Summer

Sun

Autumn

6

North Pole

Northern hemisphere

Equator

Southern hemisphere

South Pole

If you live in the northern hemisphere, or northern half of the Earth, it's summer when the **North Pole** is tilted towards the Sun. The days are long and sunny and the nights are short.

If you live in the **southern hemisphere**, summer is when the **South Pole** is tilted towards the Sun.

Winter

summer fact

At lunchtime on a summer day, your shadow looks very short. This is because the Sun is high in the sky.

Do you like playing outdoor games in summer?

In summer, the daylight lasts longer than in winter. It may still be light when you go to bed.

Around the world

Summer doesn't happen at the same time all over the world. If you live in America, Europe, India or anywhere in the northern hemisphere, summer is in June, July and August.

But in the southern hemisphere, in South America or Australia, summer is in December, January and February.

Some countries are very wet in summer. In India and other parts of Asia, the rainy **monsoon** season starts in July. The rain means crops and animals will have enough water. But it can cause floods too.

A monsoon rainstorm in the Philippines.

summer fact

A monsoon is a strong wind that blows rain clouds on to India and other parts of Asia.

North Pole

Equator

South Pole

At the North and South Poles, there are summer days when the Sun never sets and there is no night. The countries around the North Pole, such as Greenland and Iceland, are sometimes called the Land of the Midnight Sun.

In Australia, Christmas Day is usually hot and sunny. But many Australians still have snow decorations and pictures of Santa on a sleigh!

Husky dogs asleep at midnight in Greenland.

Summer weather

Many summer days are warm and sunny, with a gentle breeze to keep you cool. The Sun feels hot in summer because it's closer to us than at other times of the year.

Is there a cloud in the sky? If there is, it's probably a light, white, fluffy **cumulus cloud**. Cumulus clouds float high up and hardly ever turn into rain.

We eat cold food like ice cream and ice lollies to keep us cool.

If the sky looks dark and gloomy, there may be a **thunderstorm**. You might hear a crash of thunder and see a flash of lightning, followed by heavy rain. Lightning can strike trees and buildings.

Sometimes, summer weather is **humid**. There is no wind, and the air feels heavy, warm and damp.

Summer weather can sometimes be rainy and sunny at the same time!

11

Plants in summer

Roses, daisies, buttercups and lots of other flowers bloom in summer.

Flowers need to make seeds so that new plants can grow. A special dust inside the flower called pollen travels from one plant to another. When the pollen lands on another flower, a new seed is made.

If you looked at a flower under a microscope you would see tiny grains of pollen like this.

Many flowers have a lovely smell and contain a sweet juice called nectar. Bees and other insects smell the scent and come to collect the tasty nectar. At the same time, they carry pollen from one flower to the next.

A meadow full of sweet-smelling flowers attracts many insects in the summer.

Plants soak up light from the Sun in their leaves. The leaves use the sunlight to make food for the plant, using water from the soil and carbon dioxide from the air. This is called **photosynthesis**.

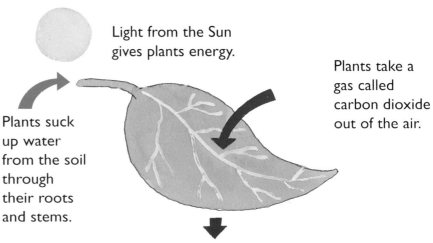

Light from the Sun gives plants energy.

Plants take a gas called carbon dioxide out of the air.

Plants suck up water from the soil through their roots and stems.

When a leaf is making food, it breathes out a gas called oxygen.

Insects like this swallowtail butterfly love to drink the sweet nectar from flowers.

summer fact

If you have hayfever, summer makes you sneeze! This happens because pollen floating in the air tickles the inside of your nose.

Animals in summer

There are more animals around in summer, because there are lots of leaves and flowers for them to eat.

Buzzard

Birds of prey, like this **buzzard**, circle in the sky looking for small animals to catch.

Jackrabbits

In rocky places, lizards and snakes **bask** in the Sun. They need its heat to warm them up.

Lizard

Bees spend the summer collecting nectar from flowers and turning it into honey. They store the honey so they will have food for the winter.

Some animals can feel too hot in the Sun. They need to cool down. Penguins don't like the heat. They spend summer days in the water and only come ashore in the evening.

King penguins coming out of the sea.

summer fact

During the summer, birds replace all their feathers! The feathers fall out two at a time, and new ones grow in their place.

On hot, sunny days, birds splash in streams and bird baths to cool down.

On the farm

Summer is a busy time for farmers. Their crops are growing tall and ripe, ready for the **harvest**. But that means birds, insects and other animals will try to eat them. How can farmers keep their crops safe?

Farmers often spray their crops with chemicals called pesticides. They keep crops safe by killing insects.

A helicopter sprays pesticide on apple trees.

Some farmers put hunting insects, such as ladybirds, in their fields. The hunters eat the smaller insects that feed on the crops.

In some hot places, such as Israel and Australia, farmers have to water their crops to make sure they don't die. This is called irrigation.

The plants in this nursery are watered with sprinklers.

Farmers put scarecrows in fields to frighten birds away. But the birds soon get used to them!

summer fact

When sunflowers are growing, they turn to face the Sun as it moves across the sky.

People in summer

Summer means fun! It's time to play outside, have picnics and go to the seaside.

Roads and airports are very busy, because so many people go on holiday at the same time.

These boys in Saudi Arabia wear white shirts that help them stay cool in the hot Sun.

Some people have **barbecues** in the garden.

Gardeners mow their lawns and water their plants.

summer fact

Wearing white or pale clothes keeps you cool, because the colour **reflects** the Sun's heat.

18

It's great fun playing in a paddling pool or having a water fight.

What special clothes do you wear in summer?

When it's really hot, all you want to wear are shorts and a T-shirt, or a sundress.

Your body uses sunshine to make vitamin D. This vitamin helps to keep your bones and teeth strong.

But the Sun can dazzle your eyes. A sunhat and sunglasses keep you in the shade.

Sandals or flip-flops let your toes stay cool.

Summer festivals

Midsummer is a holiday in many countries in the northern hemisphere. Midsummer's Day is on 21 June.

Some people like to stay up all night and watch the sun rise on midsummer morning.

summer fact

In Finland, the midsummer **festival** is marked with bonfires, flower decorations and waving flags.

In America 4 July is Independence Day. People celebrate the day when America stopped being ruled by Britain, and became a free country. There are street parties with fireworks and marching bands.

A powwow dance in Washington, USA.

Native Americans hold festivals called powwows in summer. At a powwow, there are games and sports, and **traditional** music and dancing. Powwow dancers wear costumes made of feathers.

21

Summer long ago

On a hot summer's day, everyone wants an ice cream or a cold drink from the fridge. But long ago, there were no electric fridges or freezers!

Instead, food was kept cool using ice from ice farms. These were farms where ice was collected in the winter and stored in a barn. In summer you could buy a block of ice and put it in your ice box – a kind of early fridge. The ice slowly melted as the summer went on.

These people, called Druids, meet at Stonehenge every year.

Prehistoric people celebrated midsummer. We can tell this from ancient stone circles such as Stonehenge in England. It is built so that the Sun shines through a gap in the stones on the morning of Midsummer's Day.

The Aztecs, who lived in Mexico about 500 years ago, believed the Sun was a powerful god. They worshipped him all year round, but especially at midsummer. They made human **sacrifices** to keep the Sun god happy.

An ancient Aztec temple in Mexico.

summer fact

Some Aztec people still live in Mexico. They welcome the **summer solstice** by banging drums and shaking rattles.

Summer dangers

Have fun in the summer, but watch out! The Sun and the seaside can be dangerous. But you can stay safe.

If you stay out in the Sun for too long, you might become sunburned. Your skin will look red and feel sore. Sometimes the sore skin peels off.

Rub suncream on your skin to stop sunburn.

Wear a hat and a T-shirt to keep the sun off.

If you are sunburned, stay in the shade.

At the beach, strong **currents** can sweep swimmers out to sea. Lifeguards keep watch at the seaside so they can rescue anyone who's in trouble.

Don't swim near sharp rocks like these!

Flags like these show you where it's safe to swim and paddle.

If the weather is very hot and dry, there is a **drought**. Crops can't get enough water, so they wither away and die.

Sunflowers drooping in a drought.

Summer activities

Here are some activities to do in summer.

When you're getting ready for a picnic, try these ideas.

Make quick picnic 'sausages' by rolling up a piece of ham or lettuce and a cheese slice inside a piece of soft sliced bread.

Use a cocktail stick to keep them rolled up until you eat them.

Put ice cubes in your juice or lemonade. By the time you have your picnic, the cubes will have melted, but your drink will be ice-cold.

If you have a garden, why not eat outside?

You've probably thought of making a sandcastle when you're at the beach. But how about making something else? Here are some ideas.

A sandman is like a snowman, but made out of sand. You could use shells or pebbles for his eyes and nose. Ice lolly sticks make great spiky hair.

Shells make great sandcastle decorations.

Build a sand boat or car that you can sit inside. Make a control panel out of shells and stones.

Summer experiments

Disappearing tricks

When you hang washing out to dry in the sun, where does all the water go?

It turns into a gas called water vapour and floats away into the air. This is called **evaporation**.

Try this experiment. It works best on a really hot day.

Pour about half a cup of water on a hard, flat, dry patch of ground.

When the water has spread out, draw around the wet area with a piece of chalk.

After a few minutes, look at the chalk mark again. Is the area inside it still all wet?

Some of the water has gone because it has evaporated into the air. The heat from the Sun and the ground turn the water into **vapour**.

Pupil test

Your **pupils** are the black dots in the middle of your eyes. They are holes that let light into your eyes, so that you can see.

In bright sunshine, your pupils become smaller so that they don't let in too much light.

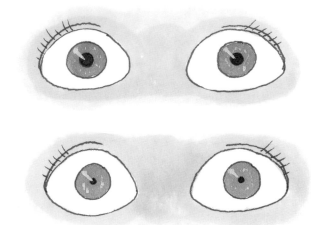

Try this experiment with your friends when you're outside on a sunny day.

Ask your friends to shut their eyes and cover them with their hands for a few seconds.

Then ask them to take their hands away quickly and open their eyes, while you watch closely.

Can you see their pupils shrink when they sense the bright sunshine?

Words to remember

barbecue
A grill for cooking food outdoors.

bask
When an animal basks, it lies in the Sun to get warm.

bird of prey
A bird that hunts and eats other animals.

bloom
When a tree or plant blooms, its flowers come out.

buzzard
A kind of bird. Buzzards hunt other birds and small animals.

cumulus cloud
A white, fluffy cloud which you can often see in summer.

current
A stream of moving water in a river or in the sea. A strong current can sweep you away.

drought
Very dry weather with little rain.

equator
The line around the middle of the Earth. There is no real line there – it is drawn on maps and globes.

evaporate
When water evaporates, it changes from a liquid into a gas and escapes into the air.

festival
A party or feast to celebrate a special date.

harvest
The time when farmers collect, or harvest, their crops.

hemisphere
One half of the Earth.

humid
When the air is very still, and feels warm and damp.

monsoon
A summer wind that brings heavy rain to India and nearby countries.

Native Americans
The people who lived in America before explorers arrived from Europe.

nectar
A sweet juice found inside flowers.

northern hemisphere
The northern half of the world, where Europe, America and Russia are.

North Pole
The most northern place on Earth.

photosynthesis
The name for the way plants turn sunlight into food inside their leaves.

pollen
A fine yellow powder made by flowers.

prehistoric
From the time before history started to be written down.

pupil
The round black hole in the middle of your eye.

reflect
When something reflects heat or light, it means that heat or light bounces off it.

sacrifice
To give up something for someone else. Long ago, people used to make human sacrifices, which meant they killed other people to make their gods happy.

southern hemisphere
The southern half of the world, where Australia is.

South Pole
The most southern place on Earth.

summer solstice
The longest day of the year, when your part of the Earth is leaning most towards the Sun.

thunderstorm
A storm with thunder, lightning and heavy rain.

tradition
Something people have done for a long time.

water vapour
The name for water that has turned into a gas.

Index

FOOD AND CELEBRATIONS
INDIA

Sylvia Goulding

This edition published in 2008 by Wayland
(a division of Hachette Children's Books)

Wayland
Hachette Children's Books
338 Euston Road
London NW1 3BH

Wayland Australia
Level 17/207 Kent Street
Sydney NSW 2000

© 2008 The Brown Reference Group plc

The Brown Reference Group plc
First Floor
9–17 St. Albans Place
London N1 0NX
www.brownreference.com

ISBN-13: 978-0-750256-36-0

Printed in Dubai

Wayland is a division of Hachette Children's Books,
an Hachette Livre UK Company.
www.hachettelivre.co.uk

10 9 8 7 6 5 4 3 2 1

Photographic Credits:
Front Cover: Fotolia: Colinda McKie (inset);
Klaus Arras (main)
Back Cover: Klaus Arras
Alamy: P. Kapoor 29, Mehdi Chebil 36; **Corbis:** Ric
Ergenbright 18; **Fotolia:** Colinda McKie 34; **iStock:** title
page, 6, 16, 31, 40; **Shutterstock:** 4, 5, 7, 8, 9, 10, 12, 13,
14, 20, 22, 23, 28, 29, 30, 32, 37, 38, 39

With thanks to models:
Anouk, Bundhalee, Caspar, Fidan, Hannah

Cooking Editor
Angelika Ilies has always been interested in cookery
and other countries. She studied nutritional sciences
in college. She has lived in the United States, England
and Germany. She has also traveled extensively and
collected international recipes on her journeys.
Angelika has written more than 70 cookbooks and
cooking card series. She currently lives in Frankfurt,
Germany, with her two children and has spent much
time researching children's nutrition. Both children
regularly cook with their mother.

Project Editor: Sylvia Goulding
Cooking Editor: Angelika Ilies
Contributors: Carey Denton, Jacqueline Fortey,
    Sylvia Goulding
Photographers: Klaus Arras, Emanuelle Morgan,
    Dirk Scholz
Cartographer: Darren Awuah
Art Editor: Paula Keogh
Illustrator: Jo Gracie
Picture Researcher: Mike Goulding
Managing Editor: Bridget Giles
Production Director: Alastair Gourlay
Editorial Director: Lindsey Lowe
Children's Publisher: Anne O'Daly

Contents

A trip around
INDIA

India has many states. Its people speak different languages, observe different religions and celebrate different festivals. They all enjoy delicious food.

India is the world's seventh largest country. It is about three-quarters the size of whole European Union. India is shaped roughly like a triangle. At the 'top' is the snow-covered Himalayas mountain range. From there it stretches southwards into the Indian Ocean, with the Arabian Sea in the west and the Bay of Bengal in the east. India shares borders with Pakistan in the north-west; with China, Bhutan and Nepal in the north; with Myanmar in the east; and with Bangladesh in the east.

The capital is New Delhi. It is in the larger urban area called Delhi. Other important cities are Mumbai (Bombay), Kolkata (Calcutta), Chennai (Madras), Bangalore and Hyderabad.

A variety of climates

India's climate is mainly tropical. This means that it is always fairly hot, and the winters are dry. The monsoon is a torrential rain that brings much-needed water for people and crops. There are four seasons: winter, summer, monsoon season in the south-west, and the after-the-monsoon season.

> ◁ **More than 1.1 billion people** live in India. That's one-sixth of all the people on Earth! Hindi is the official language of all India. Hinduism is India's main religion.

6

India is a country in Asia. It lies entirely in the northern hemisphere. It stretches from the Himalayan mountains in the north to the Indian Ocean in the south.

EUROPE
ASIA
AFRICA
INDIA

1

The Ganges is a large river in northern India. To Hindus, it is sacred. They believe that bathing in the river washes away their sins.

CHINA

Indus

PAKISTAN

HIMALAYAS

NEPAL

NEW DELHI

2

Jaipur

Agra

Ganges

1

BHUTAN

INDIA

BANGLADESH

4

Kolkata
(Calcutta)

MYANMAR

*ARABIAN
SEA*

4

INDIA

Mumbai
(Bombay)

2

GOA

Hyderabad

*BAY OF
BENGAL*

3

Bangalore

Chennai
(Madras)

Mumbai is India's largest city. Eighteen million people live here. Kolkata is the second largest city and New Delhi, the capital, the third.

SRI LANKA

△ *The Taj Mahal* is India's most famous building. It was built nearly 400 years ago by Shah Jahan, as a memorial for Mumtaz Mahal, his favourite wife.

▷ *This hotel* stands on the beach in Goa, in western India. Goa was once ruled by the Portuguese. Many Goans are Christians. Today, Goa's wonderful sandy beaches attract tourists from far away.

3

Northern India

The great Himalayas stretch across several countries. A large part of the range lies in northern India. The third tallest mountain on Earth, Kanchenjunga (8,598 m), is in the Indian Himalayas. Most of the peaks are covered in snow all year round. Many of India's major rivers, the Indus, the Ganges and the Brahmaputra, rise in these mountains.

At the south-western tip of north India is the state of Rajasthan, with the great city of Jaipur. In the south-east of north India is the state of Uttar Pradesh. Here, is the town of Agra, with the Taj Mahal memorial. Between Rajasthan and Uttar Pradesh are the states of Haryana and Delhi, with the capital New Delhi.

The plains

Most of India's north, centre and east is a vast, fertile and almost treeless plain. Millions of Indians live here and rely on the water of the great rivers from the Himalayas. There is also plenty of groundwater in the plains. This makes the land easy to water, and so much of India's food is grown on the plains.

The River Ganges flows eastwards into the Bay of Bengal. Its delta (or mouth) covers a large area. The area is shared by India and Bangladesh. The vast city of Kolkata is located in this low-lying wetland. The delta often gets flooded, and it also suffers terrible hurricanes known as typhoons.

The River Indus flows from the Himalayas through the country of Pakistan. It then enters India and ends in the Arabian Sea. The course of the Brahmaputra is from Tibet through India into Bangladesh.

▽ **This pleasant lake** is in Jammu and Kashmir, an area that is controlled by India. Other parts of Kashmir are controlled by Pakistan and China. Each of these three countries believes it should control the entire Kashmir region.

South India

South of the river plains lies the Deccan Plateau. Between this highland and the coasts are two mountain ranges. The Eastern Ghat mountain range is in the east and the Western Ghat mountain range is in the west.

This part of India has a tropical climate – it is always lush, green, and humid. Many wildlife reserves are in the South, and India's only rain forest is also here.

▽ *Musicians play traditional instruments* in Rajasthan, a state in India's northwest. People make music and sing, dance and tell poems. Folk songs tell of heroic deeds and love stories.

DO YOU SPEAK HINDI?

More than 1,000 different languages are spoken in India! Each state has its own official language. The official language of the Union of all Indian states is Hindi. Some important Indian state languages are: Assamese, Bengali, Gujarati, Hindi, Kannada, Kashmiri, Konkani, Malayalam, Marathi, Oriya, Punjabi, Sanskrit, Sindhi, Tamil, Telugu, Urdu. Many people also speak English.

The food we grow in
INDIA

Two-thirds of all people in India work on farms. India is one of the world's main food producers.

In recent years, much more food has been grown in India than before. Farmers sow better seeds, and they use more fertilisers. They water the plants in dry times and drain the land during floods. This has helped crops to grow. India sells exotic fruits and vegetables, spices and tea to other countries.

Food staples

The northern Indian state of Punjab is one of the most fertile areas in the world. It is known as India's 'bread-basket' because most of India's wheat grows here. People in northern India make flour from the wheat and bake many different kinds of bread, called chapati, naan, roti or paratha. In southern India, the farmers grow more rice. Here, people prefer rice instead of bread with their meals.

The north-western state of Rajasthan borders Pakistan. Here most oilseeds are grown. Spices are mainly cultivated in the south, especially in the state of Kerala.

Tea and coffee are other important Indian products. Sugarcane and potatoes are also grown in many parts of India.

Keeping animals

In the countryside, many Indians keep cattle for milk. Many people do not own a tractor, so they also use cattle to plough the fields. People who follow the Hindu religion do not slaughter cattle and do not eat beef. But they do keep buffaloes. Buffaloes give milk and work the fields. When they are too old, they are slaughtered and eaten.

Pulses

People in India also grow many pulses – lentils, peas and beans. These foods are good to grow for many reasons. Pulses contain many proteins. This makes them an ideal alternative to meat for India's many vegetarians. They are made into *dhals (see pages 16–17)*, and these are an important part of people's diet. Pulses are also an important fodder for cattle. And pulses are good for the soil in which they grow, too.

There are many different types of pulses. In India, the most important ones are green beans (mung beans), black matpe or urad beans, pigeon peas (arhar peas, tur peas), chickpeas, green peas, as well as all the different types of lentils.

Tea grows in three main regions in India: Darjeeling tea grows in the foothills of the Himalayas; Assam, or breakfast tea, grows in the moist, fertile lowlands around the river Brahmaputra; and Nigiril tea flourishes in the hilly Blue Mountains in the South.

A CUP OF SPICE

Masala Chai is a popular tea - chai is the Indian word for 'tea', and masala means 'spice'. To make the tea spicy, cloves, cinnamon, nutmeg, ginger, cardamom or pepper is added to the tea leaves.

The spices

A wonderful variety of colourful and fragrant spices grows in India. Spices were once very valuable. The Portuguese, the Dutch and the British took control of India centuries ago, so they could get these spices for themselves.

Among the many aromatic spices grown in India are: ajwain, aniseed, cardamom, celery, chilli, cinnamon, clove, coriander, cumin, dill seed, fennel, fenugreek, garlic, ginger, mustard, nutmeg, pomegranate seed, saffron, tejpat, turmeric and vanilla.

Meals are cooked with many different spices and spice mixes. *Garam masala* is a typical spice mixture. It means 'hot spices'. But spices are not only used to flavour food. They also have medicinal properties – some aid digestion, others can help cure a cold, for example. Spices are also used to make cosmetics and soaps.

Competition has made life difficult for small spice farms. When other countries offer the same spice at a lower price, Indian farmers lose business. So some Indian farmers have started to grow new types of spices. They might start growing vanilla instead of chillies, for example, or they may grow organic spices.

Fish and seafood

India has long coastlines and many rivers. People have fished along India's coasts for thousands of years. Many only had small boats and no modern equipment, so their catch was low. Some fishermen have set up co-operatives to share expensive equipment.

India's most important fishing region is the southern state of Kerala. Inland rivers and lakes also have fresh fish, such as trout. And fish are also bred in fish farms. One of India's most important products is prawns. These feature in many Indian dishes, for example in coconut pilau from Kerala.

◁ **Chilli is one** of seventy-five different spices that are grown in India. More spices come from India than from any other country in the world. After picking, the chillies have to be sorted, spread out to dry, and then packaged.

Fishermen sell their catch in the city of Kochi, in south-western India. Fish and seafood are sold in local markets. Families get there early to buy the freshest fish of the day. Kochi is an important fishing port.

SACRED COWS

In India, cows are everywhere. They wander the streets and do not worry about the traffic. This is because people who follow the Hindu religion believe that cows are sacred animals. So Hindus do not slaughter cattle, and they do not eat beef or veal.

let's make...
GARAM MASALA

Garam means 'hot', and *masala* means 'spices'. So this is a hot spice mixture! Every region and every family in India has its own special recipe for combining spices; here is one.

WHAT YOU NEED:

MAKES 1 SMALL JAR OF POWDER:

1 tablespoon cumin seeds
2 tablespoons coriander
 seeds
1 tablespoon cardamom
 pods
1 tablespoon peppercorns
1–2 dried chillies
2 cinnamon sticks
1 teaspoon cloves
1 bay leaf
½ teaspoon ground mace

◁ Traditional spice mixtures in India include twenty or more different spices. But even a basic mix will give your dishes a special Indian flavour.

How DO I USE garam masala?

Garam masala is a spice mixture. It is used for cooking savoury Indian dishes. It can be used in two ways: it is either fried at the beginning of cooking a dish, or it is sprinkled in at the end.

1 Heat a dry frying pan over a medium heat without adding any fat. Add the cumin and coriander seeds, the cardamom, peppercorns, chillies, cinnamon sticks and cloves.

2 Dry-roast the spices for a few minutes, stirring them with a spoon so they don't burn.

3 Allow the spices to cool a little, then crush them with a pestle in a mortar or grind them in a spice mill. Stir in the mace.

4 Put the spice mix into a container with a lid and keep it in a cool, dark place. It will last for several weeks.

To MAKE *Sambar masala*

In a dry frying pan, dry-roast 10 tablespoons coriander seeds, 8–10 dried chillies, 1 teaspoon cumin seeds, 1 teaspoon black peppercorns and 1 teaspoon fenugreek over a medium heat for a few minutes. Put the roasted spices into a bowl. Now dry-roast 1 teaspoon each of split white beans, yellow mung beans and yellow split peas for a few minutes, stirring so they won't burn. Add them to the spices. Turn off the heat. Grind or pound the spices and pulses as above. Warm 2 tablespoons ground turmeric in the still-warm frying pan and stir into the powder.

let's make...
LENTIL DHAL

A *dhal* can be two things: pulses that have been shelled and split, or a stew made from the pulses. In southern India, many people are vegetarian. They particularly love dhals.

WHAT YOU NEED:

TO SERVE 4 PEOPLE:

300g yellow split
   lentils
salt, black pepper
1 red and 1 green pepper
1 bunch spring onions
3 garlic cloves
3 red chillies
2 tablespoons ghee or
   cooking oil
1 teaspoon each garam
   masala *(see pages
   14–15)*, turmeric,
   coriander seeds and
   ground cumin

◁ We eat dhal every day, even for breakfast. We eat different ones each time. Some are sweet, most are savoury. Some are quite thick, others are soupy. I serve dhal with bread and a bowl of plain yoghurt.

WHAT'S THIS: dhal?

Dhal means 'pea' or 'lentil'. In the West, we call them pulses. There are more than seventy different types in India. They are hulled, which means their shell has been removed. And they are split. Try these in your cooking:
- chana dhal (split chickpeas)
- masoor dhal (red lentils)
- mung dhal (mung beans)
- muth dhal (brown-green beans)
- rajma dhal (kidney beans)
- urad dhal (urad or black gram, a bit like black lentils)

1 Wash the lentils. Pick over them and throw away any that look a different colour or empty.

3 Meanwhile, wash and trim the vegetables. Cut the peppers into thin strips and the spring onions into thin rings.

2 Put the good lentils into a saucepan with 600ml cold water. Add ½ teaspoon salt and grind in lots of pepper. Bring to the boil. Cover the pan, reduce the heat to low and cook gently for about 25 minutes. The lentils should be cooked but not too soft. **!**

4 Peel and finely chop the garlic. Trim, de-seed and chop the chillies (see page 5). **!**

5 Heat the ghee or cooking oil in a wide frying pan. Add the pepper, spring onion, garlic and chillies. Fry and stir for about 2 minutes. **!**

6 Add the spices and fry for a few seconds. Add the lentils together with their juices. Stir and heat through. Season with salt and pepper and serve. **!**

let's make...
CHAPATIS

Breads are particularly popular in northern India, where most of the country's wheat is grown. We make lots of different breads: chapatis, parathas, naans and rotis.

◁ An Indian girl mixes the flour to help her mother make chapatis. Chapatis are great for soaking up sauces and for scooping up rice and meat.

WHAT YOU NEED:

MAKES 12 CHAPATIS:

100g atta or roti flour
1 tablespoon salt
1 tablespoon cooking oil
240ml lukewarm water

WHAT'S THIS: _atta_ OR _roti flour?_

Atta is an Asian flour. It is ground from very hard durum wheat grains. Roti is a flour made from millet. You can find both in Asian supermarkets, or use wholegrain wheat flour instead.

1 Stir together the flour and the salt. Add the oil and the water. Knead to make a smooth dough. Allow the dough to rest at room temperature for at least 2 hours.

2 Divide the dough into 12 portions. Shape each portion into a ball. On the floured work surface, roll out each ball to make a circle of about 100mm.

4 Heat a cast-iron frying pan without oil. One at a time, put the circles into the frying pan. Cook them for a few seconds on both sides until they puff up and start showing small brown spots.

3 Thinly dust the dough circles with flour so they don't stick together. Pile them all on top of each other.

5 Once cooked, put all the chapatis into a basket and wrap them in a clean teatowel to keep them warm.

How we celebrate in
INDIA

India is a land of many festivals: every occasion is celebrated with great spectacles, special food and rituals.

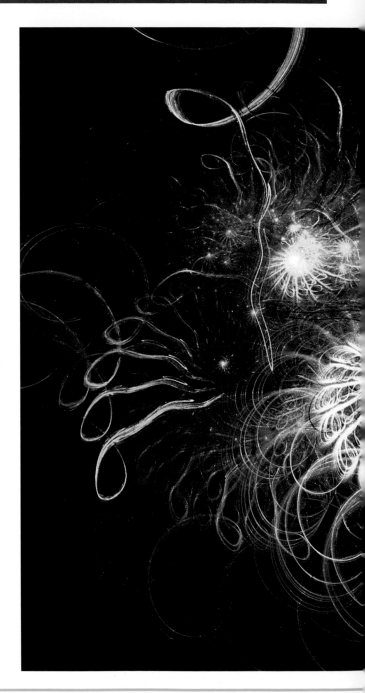

There are festivals to mark the different seasons or the arrival of the full moon. Religious festivals honour India's many gods and goddesses, or they remember an important mythological event. National festivals celebrate the founding of modern India. Some holidays are celebrated all over the country, but they have different names in different states. People also eat different festive foods to celebrate.

Independence Day

All Indians celebrate the creation of modern India. On 15 August, people remember the day India gained independence from Great Britain in 1947. They raise the Indian flag in schools and offices and sing the national anthem. Friends and families get together and share lunch or dinner. There are also many kite-flying competitions around the country.

Another national holiday is Gandhi Jayanti on 2 October. It honours Mahatma Gandhi, the great political and spiritual leader of the non-violent movement for independence from Britain. Gandhi inspired many others. He is known as the 'Father of the Indian Nation'.

Diwali – The Festival of Lights

Diwali is properly called Deepavali. The festival was originally celebrated by followers of the Hindu, Sikh and Jain religions. But the celebrations are so enjoyable that people of other faiths also celebrate Diwali.

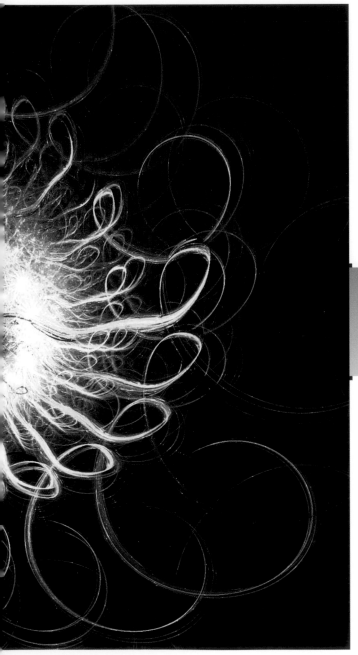

There are many different stories about the origins of Diwali. One of the most widely believed stories tells of the battle between Rama and Ravana. Lord Rama is a Hindu god. His enemy, Ravana, had kidnapped Rama's wife. But Lord Rama won the battle. Diwali remembers his victory. At the same time, it is the victory of good over evil. It also marks the victory of light over darkness.

Diwali is celebrated over five days in October or November each year. To celebrate the triumph of light, people light clay lamps called *dipa* or *deeya*. They also set off amazing fireworks all over India. People clean their homes, feast together, have fun fairs and give each other gifts. Special Diwali sweets are made or bought for the day. *Barfi* are made from condensed milk and sugar, and *badam barfi* are made with rosewater and almonds.

Diwali fireworks are lit in every area neighbourhood. There are spinning fire circles called *zameen chakra* and huge fire mountains called *anaar*. Lots of noisy fire crackers and rockets are lit in every street.

BRIGHT LIGHTS

On one of the days of the Diwali festival, many lamps are lit. The lamps make each home look bright, and the streets are also festively lit. Light symbolises knowledge. Lighting many lamps celebrates an end to ignorance.

Ramzan Id

Muslims are the second largest religious group in India. The most important Muslim celebration in India comes at the end of the month of Ramzan. (Ramzan is often known as Ramadan elsewhere.) During Ramzan, people follow a strict fast for a whole month – they do not eat or drink anything during the day. But they may eat and drink at night, between sunset and sunrise. Often, people share the first meal after the daily fast with family and friends. This meal is known as *iftaar*.

At the end of the month of fasting there are great celebrations, called Ramzan Id, or Ramzan Eid or Id-ul-Fitr. Muslims pray together and give alms (gifts) to the poor. People dress up, visit family and friends and go to fairs. Children often get *eidee* – special

△ *This statue* in New Delhi shows the Hindu god Lord Shiva. Each religious group in India has its own gods and goddesses, and their great deeds are celebrated.

△ *For the Holi Festival*, this girl has had plenty of coloured powders thrown at her. Women and men often wear white clothes so the colours show up well. They dance and sing and hug and wish each other 'Happy Holi'.

holiday money to buy toys and trinkets. The favourite Ramzan Id snack is *seviyan*, a sweet vermicelli dessert with nuts and raisins.

The Holi Festival

Holi, or the festival of colours, is another Hindu festival that has become popular with other faiths. It marks the end of winter and the arrival of spring. People celebrate the new, green growth of leaves and the colourful flowers and blossom of the trees.

To celebrate these spring colours, people throw coloured powders and water at each other. Everyone tries to look as colourful as possible. Old people join in as much as the young. The powders were originally made from natural herbs. As well as providing decoration, they were meant to protect people from spring flu and colds. Today the powders are made from artificial colours.

GLITTERING SWEETS

Festival sweets are sometimes made to look extra special with an edible silver or gold leaf.

let's make...
VEGETABLE CURRY

For festivals such as Diwali we usually eat vegetarian food. We use as many different vegetables as possible to make a curry – this is symbolic for having plentiful food all year round.

WHAT YOU NEED:

SERVES 4 PEOPLE:

150g dried black-eyed beans, soaked in water overnight
1 onion
2 garlic cloves
25mm piece fresh ginger
675g vegetables (as many different types as possible, for example baby corn, carrots, okra, spring onions, tomatoes)

3 tablespoons cooking oil
1–2 tablespoons garam masala
300ml hot water
salt, black pepper
2 tablespoons fresh coriander leaves

◁ This is a satisfying meal and delicious too. Serve it with rice or some Indian breads to soak up the sauce.

WHAT'S THIS: black-eye beans?

Black-eyed beans are also known as cowpeas. They are a good food for vegetarians because they contain lots of protein. When they are soaked and cooked, the beans swell – 150g of dried beans makes about 375g of cooked beans.

1 Drain the beans. Put them into a saucepan and cover with cold water. Bring to the boil. Drain in a sieve and refresh the beans under cold running water.

2 Return the beans to the saucepan and cover with water. Bring to the boil again. Reduce the heat, cover and simmer over a low heat for about 50 minutes until the beans are almost soft. Check from time to time and add more water if the beans are no longer covered with water.

3 Meanwhile, peel the onion, garlic and ginger. Finely chop the onion and the ginger. Crush the garlic. Wash and trim the other vegetables. Cut all the vegetables into bite-sized pieces.

4 Heat the oil in a deep, wide saucepan. Add the onion, garlic and ginger and fry for a few minutes, until they are a golden yellow.

5 Add the vegetables, a few at a time, starting with the hardest. Fry and stir for 2 minutes, then add more and fry and stir. Sprinkle the garam masala on top and fry for another minute. Pour in the hot water and stir.

6 Drain the beans and add them to the vegetables. Stir, cover and simmer over a low heat for 15 minutes. Season with salt and pepper. Sprinkle with coriander leaves and serve.

let's make...
SEVIYAN

After a month of fasting in Ramzan, people look forward to the big feast at the end, the Eid-ul-Fitr. The highlight is seviyan, a sweet milk and vermicelli noodle dessert.

WHAT YOU NEED:

MAKES 6-8 PORTIONS:

- 1 teaspoon green cardamom pods
- 1 tablespoon ghee or cooking oil
- 100g seviyan (thin vermicelli noodles from India or Pakistan)
- 1.7l milk
- 2 tablespoons raisins
- 1 tablespoon chopped almonds
- 1 tablespoon finely chopped pistachio nuts
- ½ cup sugar
- ⅛ cup cream

◁ Muslim men often give each other seviyan or other sweet dishes as a Ramzan gift. People even call the festival 'sweet Eid' because of this dish.

WHAT'S THIS: *ghee?*

Ghee is a clarified butter – it contains no particles or water. To make ghee, butter is simmered until all the water is gone. You can usually find ghee in the ethnic section of your supermarket. You can use cooking oil as a substitute.

1 Break open the cardamom pods. Ease out all the seeds and chop them with a large knife.

2 ! Heat the ghee or cooking oil in a saucepan. Add the cardamom seeds and fry them for a few seconds. In a separate pan, heat the milk (make sure it doesn't boil over!).

3 Break the noodles into smaller pieces. Add them to the pan with the ghee and the spices. Over a medium heat, fry them lightly for a few minutes, or until they are a light brown colour.

4 ! Pour in the hot milk. Bring to the boil. Reduce the heat and simmer for about 5 minutes, stirring all the time, so it doesn't burn.

5 ! Stir in the raisins, almonds and pistachios. Allow everything to simmer for about 15 minutes, until the mixture has thickened a little. Stir often so it doesn't stick to the bottom.

6 Take the saucepan off the heat. Stir the sugar and the cream into the mixture. Decorate. Serve hot or cold – the seviyan thickens as it cools.

How we celebrate at home in
INDIA

Family ties are very important in India. All celebrations are held with the entire family. People visit their relations and they share a festive meal. Often they give each other gifts of sweets and nuts.

Birthdays

Like children all over the world, children in India enjoy celebrating their birthdays. Hindu children often get a new outfit to wear on this special day. If their birthday is on a school day, they take sweets into school to hand out to their classmates. At home they enjoy a delicious meal with their family, maybe a curry dish. It is followed by the special birthday dessert, *dudh pakh*, a spiced rice pudding with nuts and fruit.

A birthday cake is also a must in India, and so are gifts and sometimes a party. Family and friends visit or telephone to 'wish you', which means 'happy birthday'. Muslim children may also celebrate their birthday with a cake and candles, but many Muslim

◁ **The bhindi or red dots** on this girl's head are festive marks in southern India. Drops and sparkling gems have also become fashionable. In the rest of the country, it is mainly married women who wear a *bhindi*.

families do not celebrate birthdays. They save their celebrating for the special festival of Ramzan Eid.

Children's Day is an international festival. In India, it is celebrated on 14 November, on the birthday of India's first prime minister, Jawaharlal Nehru. Nehru was often called *Chacha* (Uncle) Nehru by children. Some families hold a children's party on that day.

Rakhi

Rakhi is the celebration of the love between brothers and sisters. In India, this also includes step-brothers and step-sisters and cousins. It may even be celebrated by close family friends who are not related.

If the brother and sister can get together, there is a big ceremony. The sister paints a *tilak (see the box below)* on the brother's forehead. Then she ties on his *rakhi*, or thread bracelet. In return, the brother makes a solemn promise that he will always protect his sister. The brother's gift to his sister may simply be his blessing. But he may also give her some sweets or other gift, for example some jewellery, new clothes or money.

△ **This boy has his rakhi** tied on by his mother rather than his sister. He now gives his sister a promise. For as long as he lives, he will make sure that his sister is not in danger and that she is well looked after.

FACE-PAINTING

A tilak is a decoration on a man's forehead. It shows that he belongs to the Hindu faith. The decoration may be a horizontal or vertical line, or more than one line, a U-shape or a dot. The paint is made from red sandalwood paste, ashes, clay or turmeric powder.

△ **These schoolchildren** are at Amber Fort in Rajasthan. Once they finish their education, they will have a big party. The end of school life is a *samskara,* or a life stage, in a Hindu's life. After this stage, people are thought to be ready to get married.

After this, the sister performs *aarti*. This is a Hindu prayer that people sing on special occasions. She carries a tray holding an oil lamp, flowers and food around her brother. Then she offers him some sweets.

Food is important at rakhi. Samosas *(see pages 34–35)* are often eaten at family parties. Sweets are a traditional rakhi gift. *Ladoos* are particularly popular. These are round sweets flavoured with nuts and spices.

Life-cycle celebrations

Hindus mark the different stages of a person's life with rituals that are called *samskara*. There are sixteen different samskara celebrated during a person's life. Some mark the arrival of a new baby or when it is named. One is celebrated when a boy's hair is cut for the first time after birth.

On the first day of school, many Hindus pray to Saraswati, the Goddess of Learning. In southern India, the children celebrate the day by eating a sweet rice porridge, with raisins and nuts, called *sarkarai pongal*.

Weddings

A marriage is an important day in anyone's life. In India, it is also a life-cycle celebration or *samskara*. At a wedding, people believe, it is not only the bride and groom who are brought together, but their families as well. The celebrations can last five or seven days. The guests eat plenty of festive food together, so they can get to know each other.

Traditional weddings start with a *mehndi*, or henna party, the night before the wedding, at the bride's home. Instead of jewellery, the bride has lacy or flower patterns painted on her hands and feet. After the wedding, the bride does not have to do any work until the *mehndi* has washed off.

▽ **Mehndi** is a henna paste that is used to make patterns on the skin. It is safe and natural. The tattoos last from a few days to a month. A mixture of lemon juice and sugar is brushed on to the henna to make it set.

let's make...
TANDOORI CHICKEN

For special family celebrations, people eat this traditional chicken dish. They cook it over charcoal in a clay oven called a *tandoor*, from which the dish gets its name.

WHAT YOU NEED:

SERVES 4 PEOPLE:

2 garlic cloves
50mm piece fresh ginger
juice of 1 lemon
4 teaspoons tandoori
 spice mix
125ml low–fat yoghurt

4 chicken legs
2 whole chicken
 breasts with bones
cooking oil for
 brushing
salt

PLUS:

2 onions, cut into rings
2 teaspoons ground cumin
a little lemon juice,
 diluted with water
lemon wedges and fresh
 coriander leaves
 to garnish

◁ Tandoori chicken is my favourite! You can try tandoori lamb or tandoori prawns, too, using the same method.

WHAT'S THIS: *tandoori spice mix?*

Tandoori spice mix combines many spices – cardamom, cinnamon, cloves, coriander, cumin, ginger, nutmeg, paprika, pepper, salt and turmeric. Red paprika and yellow turmeric make the mixture orange in colour. Some shop-bought mixes include food colouring.

1 Peel and finely chop the garlic and ginger and put them into a bowl. Add the spices and yogurt, and stir well to combine. **!**

2 Wash the chicken legs and breasts under running cold water, then pat them dry with paper towels, and put them into a bowl. Rub or brush with the yogurt mix. Cover the bowl and chill in the fridge for at least 12 hours.

3 Preheat the oven to 230°C (gas mark 8). Take the chicken out of the yoghurt sauce, and pat them dry with kitchen towel. Place them on a rack and roast in the oven for 20 minutes.

4 Turn the chicken pieces over, brush them with a little oil and sprinkle with salt. Cook for another 20 minutes in the oven. **!**

5 Place the cooked chicken pieces on a platter. Scatter the onion rings and cumin over the top, and drizzle with lemon juice. Garnish with lemon wedges and coriander.

SAFETY WITH chicken

- Make sure you rinse and pat dry the raw chicken with kitchen towel.
- Wash cutting boards and knives in hot water after using.
- Scrub your hands thoroughly before and after handling.
- Never ever put raw chicken and cooked chicken on the same plates or cutting boards.

let's make...
SAMOSAS

Samosas are a great snack food. They can be made with lots of different fillings. We eat them with a spicy dip or chutney – my brother always has the hottest chilli sauce with it!

WHAT YOU NEED:

MAKES 16 TO 20 SAMOSAS:

3½ tablespoons ghee or oil
225g flour

1 teaspoon salt
1 teaspoon lemon juice

FOR THE FILLING:

2 tablespoons ghee or oil
2 teaspoons garam masala
200g potatoes
1 small courgette
¼ cauliflower

1 teaspoon ground ginger
½ teaspoon turmeric
1 teaspoon Cayenne pepper
½ teaspoon ground cumin
salt

PLUS:

ghee or cooking oil
for frying

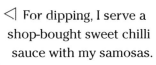

◁ For dipping, I serve a shop-bought sweet chilli sauce with my samosas.

WHAT SORT OF fillings ARE THERE FOR SAMOSAS?

North Indian or Punjabi samosas are large and plump. They often have a potato-and-pea filling with raisins or cashew nuts. Gujarati samosas are tiny and filled with lots of different vegetables. In Hyderabad, people add a spoonful of yoghurt to the samosa dough.

1 Melt the ghee and mix it with the flour, 125ml lukewarm water, salt and lemon juice. Knead for about 10 minutes to make a smooth dough. Wrap the dough in clingfilm and allow to rest for 30 minutes.

2 Make the filling. Peel and cube the potatoes. Wash, trim and cube courgette and cauliflower. Heat the ghee in a small saucepan. Add the vegetables. Fry and stir for 2 minutes. Add the spices and fry and stir for 1 minute. Add 125ml water and cover the saucepan. Turn the heat to low and simmer for 10 minutes. Remove the lid and simmer until all the liquid is gone. Allow to cool.

3 Knead the dough again, then roll it out thinly in small portions. Place a saucer (325–350mm in diameter) on top of the dough. Cut out a dough circle around the saucer. Knead the leftover dough pieces, roll them out again and cut more circles.

4 Cut each circle in half. Put 1 heaped teaspoon of filling in the centre of each half-circle. Moisten the edges with water. Fold one corner on top of the other *(see above)*. Gently squeeze the straight and the round edges together.

5 Heat the ghee or oil in a frying pan. Fry the samosas, a few at a time, for 2 minutes. Carefully turn them over and fry for 2 more minutes. Lift them out with a slotted spoon and drain on kitchen paper.

35

How we live in
INDIA

India is a country of vast contrasts. It has huge sprawling cities and tiny villages. It invents the very latest in technology. But some people still live in very traditional ways. India has international airports and bullocks pull carts through the busy city streets. There are some very rich and many very poor people.

computer programs and systems. Some Indians work in call centres or science centres for companies in other countries. They have well-paid jobs and live in brand-new flats. But many others live in poverty. Their houses are made from scrap materials. And thousands of Indians have to beg and sleep on the streets.

City life

Many young people leave the villages to find work in the cities. Some cities have new offices where people write and install new

▽ **The Cyber Gateway** is a futuristic office building in Hyderabad in eastern India. A whole area is called HITEC city. Companies that make new computer and science products are based here.

△ *An Indian woman* in a village sells traditional handicrafts. Indians produce beautiful silk and cotton clothes, colourful rugs and carpets, and attractive silver and fashion jewellery.

Village life

The majority of Indian people live in small villages. Many villages now have electricity, and some have piped water. In other villages, the people dry cow dung to use as fuel for cooking. Women get water from a well and carry it home in buckets on their heads. They wash their clothes at a nearby river or stream.

Many people in the villages belong to a cooperative. They share tools and machines. They may work together at a dairy farm or at a leather factory, or grow trees, or make mobile phones, for example. They all share the work and the money they make.

For entertainment, the people who own a television may invite their neighbours to watch with them. People also get together to chat.

School life

Children go to school from 9 A.M. until 1 P.M., older children until 3 P.M. Most take a packed lunch – often rice, chapatis and vegetables. In the villages, school may be in the open air or in one room with an earth floor. In the cities there are good state and private schools.

All children in India have to go to school between the ages of six and fourteen. But many cannot afford to go there if the journey is

△ **Street vendors** sell vegetables straight from their farm. Popular varieties are okra, tomatoes, potatoes, aubergine, squashes, carrots and onions. Many Indians are vegetarians, and vegetables are cheap.

too far away to travel to every day. Children often need to look after younger brothers and sisters. Many children have to help their families or earn money.

Family life

It is common for several generations to live together in India. Grandparents, uncles and aunts and cousins may all live together in the same house. When a man gets married, his wife comes to live in his family's house. But in the cities, the space is cramped. Often it is not possible for so many people to live together.

Mealtimes are family time. A *thali* is a common meal in India. It is named after the silver tray it is served on. Different sections of the tray hold rice, chapatis, chutney and a curry such as a vegetable curry or *rogan josh. Dhal* is another popular dish. This stew is made with spiced lentils or beans. It is an important dish for vegetarians because it has plenty of protein. Indians enjoy a cooling yoghurt drink called *lassi* or fresh fruit juices.

▽ **Indian Railways** runs one of the largest and busiest railway networks in the world. It is also the largest employer in the world – more than one million people work on the trains.

Time off

Going to the cinema is the most popular way to spend spare time in India. The so-called 'Bollywood' films mix adventure and love stories with song and dance. People also enjoy reading the gossip about their favourite film stars. Cricket is the top favourite sport in India. The country has many professional cricket teams, and people play cricket whenever they get a chance.

BOLLYWOOD

More films are made in India than anywhere else in the world. The film industry is called 'Bollywood' - it takes the letter 'B' from Bombay, the former name of Mumbai, and the rest from Hollywood.

let's make...
LOVELY LASSI

This is a super chilled yoghurt drink! It's refreshing on hot days, and in winter I just leave out the crushed ice. Lassi also helps cool your mouth if you are eating a very spicy dish.

▽ I just love drinking lassi!

WHAT YOU NEED:

MAKES 6-8 GLASSES:

900g yoghurt
125ml chilled water
salt
½ teaspoon ground cumin
1 teaspoon lemon juice
crushed ice
some fresh mint leaves

MY TIP

To make crushed ice, you can use an ice crusher. If you haven't got a crusher, just put all the ice cubes you need between two clean teatowels. Then pound them with a rolling pin or mallet to break up the cubes.

1 Put the yoghurt, chilled water, salt, ground cumin and lemon juice into a bowl or measuring jug. Using a spoon or a whisk, stir all the ingredients thoroughly to combine them well into a smooth mixture.

2 Half-fill the glasses with crushed ice *(see My Tip opposite)*. Pour the lassi on top of the ice. Decorate with fresh mint leaves. Cheers!

SWEET VARIATION: Mango Lassi

In a blender, purée the flesh of 1 mango with 950ml full-fat yoghurt, 240ml chilled water, and 4 tablespoons sugar. Put crushed ice into glasses and pour the mango lassi on top.

let's make...
ROGAN JOSH

This dish was originally cooked with mutton and plenty of aromatic spices. It is a classic North Indian family favourite, and every family has their own recipe.

WHAT YOU NEED:

SERVES 4 PEOPLE:

900g lamb (from the leg)
12mm piece ginger
3 garlic cloves
2 onions

5 tablespoons ghee
120g yoghurt
fresh coriander leaves
salt

FOR THE SPICE MIXTURE:

½ teaspoon ground cardamom
a pinch of ground cloves
½ teaspoon ground black pepper
a pinch of ground cinnamon

1 teaspoon hot paprika
1 teaspoon ground coriander
1 teaspoon ground cumin

◁ Serve the rogan josh with boiled rice or with chapatis *(see pages 18–19).*

WHAT'S THIS: _mutton?_

Mutton is from an old sheep; lambs are young sheep. Mutton has a stronger flavour, but it can be tough so it must be cooked for a long time.

MY TIP

If you can get hold of it, try cooking this dish with goat meat.

1 Wash the lamb under cold water and pat it dry with kitchen towel. Cut the meat into bite-sized chunks.

2 Peel and finely chop the ginger, garlic and onions. Combine all the spices in a small bowl. **!**

3 Heat the ghee or oil in a large saucepan. Add the meat chunks and fry them all over, stirring, until they no longer look pink. **!**

4 Take out the meat and set it aside. Add the ginger, garlic and onions. Fry for 2 minutes. Add the spice mixture, stir and fry for 2 minutes. **!**

6 Stir the curry from time to time. Add more water if it gets too dry. Garnish with fresh coriander and serve with boiled basmati rice. **!**

5 Return the meat to the saucepan. Add the yoghurt, 240ml water and 1 teaspoon salt and stir. Simmer everything over a low heat for 1 hour.

let's make...
COCONUT PILAU

This recipe is an everyday dish from the southern state of Kerala. Many dishes there are vegetarian, but seafood is also popular. Coconut is a typical local ingredient.

WHAT YOU NEED:

SERVES 4 PEOPLE:

450g basmati rice
salt
50mm piece fresh ginger
1–2 chillies
4 garlic cloves
2 teaspoons ground cumin
1 teaspoon ground cardamom
a pinch of ground cinnamon
1 large onion
3 tomatoes
2 tablespoons cooking oil
125g yoghurt
125ml unsweetened coconut milk

340g peeled cooked prawns (or firm fish fillet or cubed chicken)
2 tablespoons cashew nuts, chopped and roasted
a handful of spring onion rings

◁ I like prawns, and the bigger, the better. They're easy to shell – just pull off the head and the tail, peel the prawn open at the belly, and pull off the shell. Yummy!

WHAT'S THIS: pilau?
Pilau is originally an Arabic word. There are many different spellings and pronunciations: pilaf, pilav, pilao. The main ingredients are usually chicken or seafood. Often, coconut, nuts or dried fruits are added to the dish. It always has many spices.

1 Wash the rice in a sieve. Put it in a saucepan, add 600ml cold water and 1 teaspoon salt. Bring to the boil, stir and cover. Simmer over a low heat for 15–20 minutes. Add a little more water if it looks dry.

3 Peel and chop the onions. Chop the tomatoes. Heat the oil in a deep frying pan. Add the onion and fry it until it is golden brown.

2 Meanwhile peel the ginger and garlic. Trim and de-seed the chillies *(see page 5)*. Put ginger, garlic, chillies, cumin, cardamom and cinnamon into a cup with 3 tablespoons water. Purée with a hand-held blender or in the mixer until it is a fairly smooth paste.

4 Add the spice paste and stir well. Stir in the tomatoes, yoghurt and coconut milk. Cook over a medium heat for 10 minutes, stirring from time to time. Stir in the prawns and cook for 3–4 minutes.

5 Stir in the rice and season with a little salt. Scatter the roasted cashew nuts and onion rings over the top of the dish and serve.

Look it up
INDIA

chapati one of many different types of bread in India

chutney a dipping sauce

dhal (1) a pulse, a dried split bean or pea; (2) a stew-like dish made from pulses

Diwali the Hindu Festival of Light, one of the greatest Indian celebrations

garam masala a spice mix, literally 'hot spices'; it is often sprinkled over a dish at the end of cooking

ghee clarified butter; you can use cooking oil instead

henna a plant material used for making temporary tattoos

Holi a festival that involves throwing colour and paint over each other

mehndi (1) a temporary henna tattoo, applied to hands and feet, especially before a wedding; (2) the party, when wedding tattoos are applied

lassi a popular yoghurt drink

pulses shelled and split beans or peas commonly used in Indian cooking

samosa a deep-fried pastry triangle filled with vegetables or meat

samskara a life-cycle celebration, such as birth, name-giving, first day at school or a wedding

seviyan a sweet dessert dish, eaten or given for the Muslim festival Ramzan Eid

tandoor a clay oven; it develops great heat and is used for cooking meat dishes like tandoori chicken as well as breads

tandoori spice mix a reddish/yellowish spice mixture used to marinate chicken or other dishes before cooking in the tandoor oven

thali a silver tray used to hold several different Indian dishes or chutneys

Find out more
INDIA

Books to read

Engfer, Lee
India in Pictures (Visual Geography)
Lerner Books, 2008

Heydlauff, Lisa, and Upadyhe, Nitin
Going to School in India
Charlesbridge Publishing, 2005

Sheen, Barbara
Foods of India (Taste of Culture)
KidHaven Press: 2006

Landau, Elaine
India (True Books: Countries)
Children's Press, CT: 2000

Swan, Erin Pembrey
India (Enchantment of the World)
Children's Press,
CT, 2002

Web sites to check out

http://india.gov.in
The official Indian government site

http://india.gov.in/knowindia/kids.php
The Indian government's Kids Corner,
providing information on history, culture
and national symbols

**www.historyforkids.org/learn/india/
food/index.htm**
Information on Indian food and history,
especially for children

www.kidswebindia.com
Aimed at kids and young teens, with
information on India and its regions,
festivals, recipes, news, puzzles, gardening
advice and much more

www.pitara.com
News, puzzles, and fun relating
to India, for children

Index

INDIA